The PC
is not a typewriter

The PC
is not a typewriter

A style manual for creating
professional-level type
on your personal computer

Robin Williams

Peachpit Press
Berkeley ▪ California

Peachpit Press

2414 Sixth Street

Berkeley ▪ California ▪ 94710

510.527.8555

800.283.9444

510.524.9775 fax

The PC is not a typewriter
©1992 by Robin Williams

Appendices A through D researched and written by Ralph Wilson, edited by Robin Williams. Thanks, Ralph!

ISBN 0-938151-49-5

0 9 8 7 6 5 4 3 2 1
Printed and bound in the United States of America

To the memory of William Strunk, Jr.,
whose writings and philosophy taught
me to "make definite assertions."

*R*emember, the music is not in the piano.

—Clement Mok, *Clement Mok Designs*

Contents.

Read me first.

It has long been an axiom of mine that the little things are infinitely the most important.

Sir Arthur Conan Doyle, 1925

This phenomenon of desktop publishing is certainly incredible. Never before has professional-level type been available so readily and easily and, best of all, inexpensively—even the smallest business or the most harried college student can create high-quality pages, from annual reports to a letter for Mom to theses papers to visual presentations.

Thousands of us are circumventing the professional typesetters and creating this type ourselves, assuming that because this machine has a keyboard it works like a typewriter. Wrong. Professional typesetters know things we don't. This book does not pretend to be a treatise on design or typography or desktop publishing—there are many excellent books available in those areas. Rather, the purpose of this book is to let you in on some of the secrets that have been used for centuries to make type pleasing, beautiful, readable, legible, and artistic—secrets we just weren't taught in Typing 1A.

Many of the concepts presented in this book are subtle, yes—but they add up to a professional look. Perhaps most people couldn't put a finger on exactly what *gives* it that look, but everyone is aware of it. If we are taking type out of the hands of professionals, then we must upgrade *our* awareness of what makes their work *look* professional. It's just a matter of raising our consciousness, of looking a little closer at our printed pages with a bit more critical eye.

And of forgetting the rules our typing teachers taught us. **The PC is not a typewriter.** The type we are using is not mono-spaced, mono-weight, mono-sized, mono-boring; it's capable of being the highest quality. And, as Mies van der Rohe said, "God is in the details."

I strongly feel it is our obligation—every one of us who uses the computer to create text on a page—to uphold the highest possible level of typographic quality in this changing world.

One space between sentences.

Use only one space after periods, colons, exclamation points, question marks, quotation marks—any punctuation that separates two sentences.

What? you say! Yes—for years you've been told to hit two spaces after periods, and on a typewriter you should. But this is no typewriter.

On a typewriter, all the characters are **monospaced;** that is, they each take up the same amount of space—the letter **i** takes up as much space as the letter **m.** Because they are monospaced, you need to type two spaces after periods to separate one sentence from the next. But . . .

On a computer, most typefaces use **proportional** characters; that is, each character takes up a proportional amount of space—the letter **i** takes up about one-fifth the space of the letter **m** (except fonts like Monaco, Courier, Pica, or Elite, which are designed to emulate typewriters and why would you want to use your computer to make your work look like a typewriter?). So with proportionally-designed typefaces you no longer need extra spaces to separate the sentences. Take a careful look at these two examples:

```
Notice in this paragraph how the letters
line up in columns, one under the other,
just as on your typewriter.  This is
because each character in this font,
Courier, takes up the same amount
of space.  This monospacing is what
makes it necessary to use two spaces
to separate sentences.
```

This paragraph, however, uses a font with *proportional* spacing (Times). Each character takes up a proportional amount of the space available. Thus the single space between sentences is enough to visually separate them, and two spaces creates a disturbing gap.

Of course, this one-space rule applies just as well to the spacing after colons, semicolons, question marks, quotation marks, exclamation points, or any other punctuation you can think of. Yes, this is a difficult habit to break, but it must be done.

Take a look at any magazine or book on your shelf—you will never find two spaces between sentences (the only exception will be publications or advertisements produced on a personal computer by someone who was still following typewriter rules).

Quotation marks.

■

Use real quotation marks—never those grotesque generic marks: use " and " —not " and ".

Of course, on a typewriter when you wanted quotation marks you used the typewriter quote marks, the ones that otherwise one would think are inch marks (") and foot marks ('). Those symbols are never found, though, as quotation marks in a book, magazine, ad, poster, etc., simply because that is not what they are.

Most software programs allow you to access real quotation marks using certain keyboard combinations. The chart below provides the combinations for several programs, and you will find a more complete reference at the back of this book. It takes an extra second to access true quotation marks, but you get used to it. The subtle, added professionalism they give your work is very well worth the effort. There's no excuse for not using them. *Typewriter quotation marks are the single most visible sign of unprofessional type.*

Software package	" opening double quote	" closing double quote	' opening single quote	' closing single quote
PageMaker 4.0	Ctrl Shift [	Ctrl Shift]	Ctrl [	Ctrl]
MS Word *(Windows)*	Alt 0147	Alt 0148	Alt 0145	Alt 0146
MS Word *(DOS)*	you can't			
Ventura *(Windows)*	Alt 0147	Alt 0148	` *(under tilde~)*	'
Ventura *(GEM)*	Ctrl Shift [	Ctrl Shift]	` *(under tilde~)*	'
WordPerfect *(press Control V, then type the numbers, including the comma)*	Ctrl V 4,32	Ctrl V 4,31	Ctrl V 4,29	Ctrl V 4,28

■

There often seems to be confusion about where the quotation marks belong when there is punctuation involved. These are the guidelines:

- Commas and periods are **always** placed **inside** the quotation marks. Always. Really.*

- Colons and semicolons go **outside** the quotation marks.

- Question marks and exclamation points go **in or out,** depending on whether they belong to the material inside the quote or not. Logically, if they *belong* to the quoted material, they go *inside* the quote marks, and vice versa.

- If more than one paragraph is quoted, the double quote is placed at the beginning of each paragraph, but only at the end of the last one. What an interesting convention.

In America, that is; many other countries follow the same format for periods and commas as we do for question marks and exclamation points.

Apostrophes.

Use real apostrophes, not the foot marks: ' not '.

This is actually exactly the same as the previous chapter, but it's set off separately because it is so important and often people don't connect quotation marks with apostrophes. But the apostrophe is nothing more than the single closing quotation mark.

Repeated from the previous chapter:

Software package	' apostrophe (closing single quote)
PageMaker 4.0	Ctrl]
MS Word *(Windows)*	Alt 0146
MS Word *(DOS)*	you can't
Ventura *(Windows)*	'
Ventura *(GEM)*	'
WordPerfect	Ctrl V 4,28
(press Control V, then type the numbers, including the comma)	

Apostrophe rules

As an aside, many people are often confused about where the apostrophe belongs. There are a couple of rules that work very well:

For possessives: Turn the phrase around. Place the apostrophe after whatever word you end up with.

For example, in the phrase **the boys' camp,** to know where to place the apostrophe say to yourself, "The camp belongs to the **boys.**" So put the apostrophe after the word **boys.**

The phrase **the boy's camp** says, "The camp belongs to the **boy.**"

Another example: **the women's room;** "The room belongs to the **women.**"

The big exception to this rule for possessives is the word **its.** The word **its** used as a possessive *never* has an apostrophe! **Its** only has an apostrophe as a contraction—**it's** *always* means "it is" or "it has." **Always.**

It may be easier to remember if you recall that the possessives **yours, hers,** and **his** don't use apostrophes—and neither should **its.**

For contractions: The apostrophe replaces the missing letter.

For example: **you're** always means **you are;** the apostrophe is replacing the **a** from **are.** That's an easy way to distinguish it from **your** as in **your** house and to make sure you *don't* type: Your going to the store.

As previously noted, **it's** means "it is"; the apostrophe is indicating where the **i** is left out. **Don't** means "do not"; the apostrophe is indicating where the **o** is left out.

For omission of letters: In a phrase such as **Rock 'n' Roll**, there should be an apostrophe *before and after* the **n,** because the **a** and the **d** are both left out. And don't turn the first apostrophe around—just because it appears in *front* of the letter does not mean you need to use the opposite single quote. An apostrophe is still the appropriate mark (*not* **'n'**).

In a phrase such as **House o' Fashion**, the apostrophe takes the place of the **f.** There is no earthly reason for an apostrophe to be set *before* the **o.**

In a phrase such as **Gone Fishin'** the same pattern is followed—the **g** is missing.

In a date when part of the year is left out, an apostrophe needs to indicate the missing year. **In the 80s** would mean the temperature; **In the '80s** would mean the decade. (Notice there is no apostrophe before the **s**! Why would there be? It is not possessive, nor is it a contraction—it is simply a plural.)

Dashes.

Never use two hyphens instead of a dash.
Use hyphens, en dashes, and em dashes appropriately.

Everyone knows what a hyphen is—that tiny little dash that belongs in some words, like mother-in-law, or in phone numbers. It's also used to break a word at the end of a line, of course.

On a typewriter, we were taught to use a double hyphen to indicate a dash, like so: - - . We were taught to use a double hyphen because typewriters didn't have a real dash, as the professional typesetters have. Now we no longer need to use the double hyphen—the computer has an **em dash,** which is a long dash such as you see in this sentence. There is also an **en dash,** which is about half as long as an em dash.

Hyphen   -

A hyphen is strictly for hyphenating words or line breaks. Your punctuation style manual goes into detail about when to use a hyphen; there doesn't seem to be a great deal of confusion surrounding that issue. We all know where to find it—on the upper right of the keyboard, next to the equal sign.

En dash   –

An en dash is called an en dash because it's approximately the width of a capital letter N in that particular font and size. It is used between words **indicating a duration,** such as hourly time or months or years. Use it where you might otherwise use the word "to." The en dash can be used with a thin space on either side of it, if you want a little room, but don't use a full space. Here are a few examples of places to use the en dash. Notice that, really, these are *not* hyphenated words, and a plain hyphen is not the logical character to use.

> October – December
>
> 7:30 – 9:45 A.M.
>
> 3–5 years of age

Also use the en dash when you have a compound adjective and one of the elements is made of two words or a hyphenated word, such as:

San Francisco–Chicago flight
pre–Vietnam War period
twenty-three–purple-toed Venutians

Em dash —

The **em dash** is twice as long as the en dash—it's about the size of a capital letter M. You can often use this dash in a manner similar to a colon or parentheses, or to indicate an abrupt change in thought, or in a spot where a period is too strong and a comma is too weak (check your punctuation style manual for the exact use of the dash, if you're unsure). Our equivalent on the typewriter was the double hyphen, but now we have a real em dash.

Since you were properly taught, of course, you know that the double hyphen is not supposed to have a space on either side of it—neither is the em dash, as you can see right here in this sentence. There are six other examples of the em dash in this chapter.

Here are the keys to access the dashes in several programs. See Appendices A through D for more detailed information.

Software package	- hyphen	– en dash	— em dash
PageMaker 4.0	-	Ctrl =	Ctrl Shift =
MS Word *(Windows)*	-	Alt 0150	Alt 0151
MS Word *(DOS)*	-	*none*	Alt 196
Ventura *(Windows)*	-	Alt 0150	Alt 0151
Ventura *(GEM)*	-	Ctrl [	Ctrl]
WordPerfect	-	Ctrl V 4,33	Ctrl V 4,34
(press Control V, then type the numbers, including the comma)			

Special characters.

Take advantage of the special characters available.

Creating professional-level type right at our desktop includes the potential to use such marks as ®, ™, ¢, etc. (which are the particular topic of this chapter), as well as such luxuries as accent marks that can be placed right over the letters they belong to (dealt with in the following chapter), and real quotation marks and apostrophes (see pages 15 and 17).

Unfortunately, on DOS-based computers each software package uses a different set of key combinations to access the special characters, and then it depends on whether or not your font has these characters built in, whether your monitor can display them, and whether your printer can print them. Below is a mini-chart showing several alternate characters and how to create them in a few of the most popular packages, but you should check the appendices at the back of this book for more complete information.

Software package	• *(bullet)*	©	®	™
PageMaker	Ctrl Shift 8	Ctrl Shift o	Ctrl Shift g	*none*
MS Word *(Windows)*	Alt 0149	Alt 0169	Alt 0174	*none*
MS Word *(DOS)*	Alt 7	*none*	*none*	*none*
Ventura *(Windows)*	Alt 0249	Alt 0169	Alt 0174	Alt 0153
Ventura *(GEM)*	Alt 195	Ctrl Shift c	Ctrl Shift r	Ctrl Shift 2
WordPerfect	Ctrl V 4,0	Ctrl V 4,23	Ctrl V 4,22	Ctrl V 4,51

(press Control V, then type the numbers, including the comma)

Superscript and Subscript
Don't forget about the superscript and subscript possibilities you have. The precise method to create a super- or subscript character depends on your

application, but every software package provides a way. Here is the general idea, and you can check the appendices for the steps to use in your particular application:

- To create a superscript such as the **rd** in **3ʳᵈ,** simply do this: type **3rd**; select the **rd** and choose "superscript."

- To create a subscript such as the **2** in **H₂O,** simply do this: type **H2O**; select the **2** and choose "subscript."

If your application allows you to use a keyboard command shortcut for super- and subscripts, then use that shortcut *before* you type the character. *After* you type it, *use the same keyboard shortcut* to return to normal text. For instance, if the keyboard shortcut for superscript is Control Shift \ , then you could type the following sequence to get **3ʳᵈ place**:

type **3**	then press Control Shift \
type **rd**	then press Control Shift \
hit the *Spacebar*	then type **place**

Fractions

Ever wonder where the fractions are? There aren't any. Generally speaking, anyway—some of the newer fonts have a few of the most common. If you're writing a math book, you would probably want to invest in a specialized font that carries them all. But for occasional use, try this trick:

- Type the whole number and the fraction with no space between, like so: **21/2**.

- Select the **1** and make it a superscript.

- Select the **2** and change its size to about half the point size of the original text.

- It'll look like this: **2½.** Isn't that pretty?

  Kerning (page 29) can help adjust the numbers around the fraction bar.

Accent marks.

Where an accent mark is appropriate, use it.

We couldn't use accent marks on a typewriter, but now that we are creating professional-level type we should take advantage of using them where they are appropriate. On a PC, though, placing an accent mark directly above a character is not an obvious move. If you've ever tried to use the tilde key to type the word piñata with the tilde over the n, you've noticed that it doesn't work—you get pin~ata. That doesn't look very intelligent.

The accent marks are all hidden within the codes that you access with certain key combinations, just like the special characters I mentioned in the previous chapters. Again, the characters that are available for printing depend on a variety of factors which are more fully explained in the appendices of this book. Here is a brief list of the most common marks and the key combinations for them in a few of the programs.

Accented Character	Ventura (Windows) Word (Windows) PageMaker	Ventura (GEM) Word (DOS)	WordPerfect (type Ctrl V, the symbol shown, then a character)
é	Alt 0233	Alt 130	Ctrl V ' e
É	Alt 0201	Alt 144	Ctrl V ' E
è	Alt 0232	Alt 138	Ctrl V ` e
È	Alt 0200	Alt 201	Ctrl V ` E
ñ	Alt 0241	Alt 164	Ctrl V ~ n
Ñ	Alt 0209	Alt 165	Ctrl V ~ N
ç	Alt 0231	Alt 135	Ctrl V , c
Ç	Alt 0199	Alt 128	Ctrl V , C
ö	Alt 0246	Alt 148	Ctrl V " o
Ö	Alt 0214	Alt 153	Ctrl V " O

Underlining.

Don't underline. Underlining is for typewriters; italic is for professional text.

Have you ever seen a word underlined in a magazine or a book? Most likely not. That's because typesetters are able to *italicize* words for emphasis or for proper convention (such as book titles, periodicals, operas, symphonies).

On a typewriter, of course, we had no way to italicize. So we were taught to underline words for emphasis, or to underline those items just mentioned (books, periodicals, etc.). Since we are upgrading the quality of our type, we should follow the professional standard of italicizing those items that should be italicized.

Underlining in general should be avoided. The underline tends to be heavy, is too close to the type, and bumps into the "descenders" of the letters (those parts that hang below the line, as in the letters g, j, p, q, and y).

If you want to emphasize a word or two, you have other options also. Try **bold type,** larger type, **or a different font.**

> Simply setting a bit of text apart from the rest
> of the copy can call extra attention to it.

This doesn't mean you should never have any sort of underline with text— just don't use the underline style that appears on the menu. If you really do want the *look* of an underline, use a drawn line (called a "rule" in typesetter's jargon). Most word processors and all page layout, paint, and draw programs have some way for you to draw a line under a word or headline. When you draw a line, you can place it where you want and make it as thick or thin or long as you want. You can avoid making the line bump into the descenders. The drawn line also tends to look smoother than the underline because it is one long line, not a series of short lines hooked together.

This is an underlined phrase.

This phrase has a rule drawn under it.

This phrase has an *italic* word.

apitals.

Very rarely (almost never) use all capital letters.

On a typewriter, our only way to make a headline stand out was to type it in all caps, or maybe underline it. Now, of course, we can make the text larger, or bold, or shadowed, or outlined, or italic, or any gross combination of all those. We no longer need to rely on all caps to make something noticeable. And we shouldn't.

Many studies have shown that all caps are much harder to read. We recognize words not only by their letter groups, but also by their shapes, sometimes called the "coastline." Take a look at these words and their shapes:

cat   dog   bigger   pretty

When these words are all caps, can you tell their shapes apart?

CAT   DOG   BIGGER   PRETTY

When a word is all caps, we have to read it letter by letter, rather than by recognizing groups of letters. Try reading this block of text set in all caps; be conscious of how much slower than usual you read it and how tiring it is on your eyes.

> WEN YOU'RE A MARRIED MAN, SAMIVEL, YOU'LL UNDERSTAND A GOOD MANY THINGS AS YOU DON'T UNDERSTAND NOW; BUT VETHER IT'S WORTH WHILE GOIN' THROUGH SO MUCH TO LEARN SO LITTLE, AS THE CHARITY-BOY SAID VEN HE GOT TO THE END OF THE ALPHABET, IS A MATTER O' TASTE.
>
> Charles Dickens, *Pickwick Papers*

Setting a *strange-looking* font in all caps is particularly bad news, or setting caps in italic or calligraphy or an italic-outlined-bold-shadowed-underlined face in reverse on a patterned background—aack! Take a look at how this font in all caps becomes almost impossible to read:

COMPUTER MADNESS   (13 point, Linoscript regular)

All caps also takes up a lot more space. With lowercase letters, you can make the type size bigger and bolder in the same amount of space, which will be more efficient and more effective.

Computer Madness   (18 point, Folio bold)

Occasionally you may have some very good reason to use all caps in a very short block of text or in a heading. Sometimes the particular look you want on the page can only be created with all caps. When you do that, just be aware of the inherent problems; recognize that you're making a choice between a design solution and the legibility/readability of the piece. Be able to justify the choice.

A little puzzle

Here is a fun little teaser to impress upon you how much we depend on word shapes to read. On the following lines are two well-known proverbs. The letters are indicated only by black rectangles the size of each letter. Can you read the sentences? How quickly would you be able to read the words if they were set this way in all caps?

1. A ▉▉▉▉▉▉ ▉▉▉▉▉ ▉▉▉▉▉▉▉ ▉▉ ▉▉▉▉▉.

2. You ▉▉▉ ▉▉▉▉ ▉ ▉▉▉▉▉ ▉▉ ▉▉▉▉▉, ▉▉▉ ▉▉▉ ▉▉▉'▉ ▉▉▉▉ ▉▉▉ ▉▉▉▉▉.

erning.

Adjust the space between letters according to your sensitive visual perception.

One of the most important things a professional typesetter does for a client is **kern** the type. **Kerning** is the process of removing small units of space between letters in order to create *visually-consistent letterspacing;* the larger the letters, the more critical it is to adjust their spacing. Awkward letterspacing not only looks naïve and unprofessional, it can disrupt the communication of the words. Look carefully at these two examples (try squinting):

WASHINGTON *unkerned*

WASHINGTON *kerned*

The secret of kerning is that *it is totally dependent on your eye, not on the machine.* In the first example, each letter has mechanically the same amount of space on either side of it. Some spaces *appear* to be larger because of the shape of the letter—angled or rounded. In the second example, the computer application was set to adjust, or kern, the letters, and it did a fairly good job, but the letters still needed some manual adjusting. *Type needs a human eye for the fine tuning.*

Take a look at the square and circle below—which appears to be larger?

Actually, they are both exactly the same size from edge to edge. The circle *appears* to be smaller because of all the white space surrounding it. It is this fact that creates the need to manually and visually letterspace/kern type—each character presents a different visual impression on the page, and reacts with the other letters according to their particular combinations of dark and light space. These impressions can be broken down into a few generalized combinations:

HL   Characters with verticals next to each other need the most amount of space; this can often be used as a guideline with which to keep the spacing consistent.

HO   A vertical next to a curve needs less space.

OC   A curve next to a curve needs very little space.

OT   A curve can actually overlap into the white space under or above the bar or stem of a character, and vice versa.

AT   The closest kerning is done where both letters have a great deal of white space around them.

Remember, the point is to keep the spacing visually consistent—there should visually *appear* to be the same amount of space between all the letters. It's not critical how much—it's critical that whatever it is be consistent. You can usually focus better on that white space if you look at the text with your eyes squinted. Using the kerning function, it is possible to add or to remove tiny units of space between letters, allowing for very precise positioning.

Kerning is not possible in all applications; typically you'll find it in page layout programs or in applications where text manipulation is a primary feature. You won't usually find it possible to control the kerning in a word processor. Check the software manual for the particular method for kerning in your application.

*T*abs and indents.

Use those tabs and first-line indents regularly.
Never use the space bar to align text.

Too many people try to use the spacebar to line up words or numbers. That method works on a typewriter because every letter takes up the same amount of space, so five spaces is always five spaces. This is not true when you use proportional type (see page 13) on a personal computer. If you want text to align, you *must* use tabs.

The first-line indent marker is often overlooked. What a wonderful invention! Remember on a typewriter when you wanted to indent your paragraphs? You would set a tab for five spaces in from the left margin, and at the end of a paragraph hit the carriage return, hit the tab key, then begin typing again. Well, the first-line indent does all of that for you: when you set the indentation you want, every time you hit the Return key (only at the end of a *paragraph*, remember, not the end of every line because the type *word wraps* at the right margin), the first line of your next paragraph will automatically indent. Like so:

> There is a tide in the affairs of men, which, taken at the flood, leads on to fortune; omitted, all the voyage of their life is bound in shallows and in miseries.
> On such a full sea are we now afloat; and we must take the current when it serves, or lose our ventures.
>
> —*William Shakespeare*

These indentations were set with a first-line indent, **not** *a tab.*

You can do just the opposite to create a hanging paragraph, like so:

> The poor world is almost six thousand years old, and in all this time there was not any man died in his own person, *videlicet,* in a love-cause.
> But these are all lies: men have died from time to time and worms have eaten them, but not for love.
>
> —*William Shakespeare*

These indentations were also set using the first-line indent; the first line was set to the **left** *of the margin marker.*

■

On a PC, each software package has its own way to create the tabs and indents. For this chapter I chose PageMaker with which to illustrate the concepts. Once you understand the concepts, you will (I hope) be able to apply them using the particular tab-creating method for your particular application.

Margins and indents

In any professional-level package there is some sort of command to specify the outer **margins** of the page. When you want to set the text inward from the margin, typically you use the **indents.**

As you type, the text will begin at the left margin and continue to the right margin (or between the indents, if you have indented). When text reaches the right margin, it *automatically word-wraps* and takes itself to the next line, back to the left margin, without your having to hit a Return.

*In PageMaker, dotted lines in the ruler indicate the **margins** of the text block, and triangles indicate the **indents.***

You usually also have a **first-line indent.** As mentioned on the previous page, this is the feature that eliminates the need to hit the Tab key for paragraph indentations.

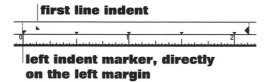

*In PageMaker, the left triangle marker splits into two parts. The top half of the triangle is the **first-line** indent. The bottom half is the **left** indent. As you type, the text bounces between the right triangle and the bottom half of the left triangle, irregardless of where the actual **margins** are.*

When you press the Return/Enter key the cursor returns to wherever you set the *first-line indent.* When the text you type reaches the right margin, it will word wrap and will align back at the point where you set the *left indent* (which, in the example above, from PageMaker, is directly on the *left margin*).

Tabs

Most programs have default tabs set about every half inch. A good program typically has at least four different sorts of tabs. Their actual appearance will vary from the PageMaker tabs shown, but they all act in a similar manner.

- **Left-aligned tab:** when you create and use a left-aligned tab, the text lines up at the tab stop and types out to the right, so the *left* side of the text is aligned.

  Typically the marker has a little tail pointing to the right, in the direction the text will type.

  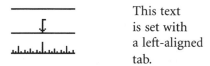

  This text
  is set with
  a left-aligned
  tab.

- **Right-aligned tab:** when you create and use a *right-aligned* tab, the text lines up at the tab stop and types out to the left, so the *right* side of the text is aligned. It actually looks like it's typing backwards.

  Typically the marker has a little tail pointing to the left, in the direction the text will type.

  This is the tab to use for columns of numbers, to keep all the ones and tens and so on in their proper columns. Also, if you want to send the date over to the right side of the page, set a right-aligned tab directly on the right margin.

  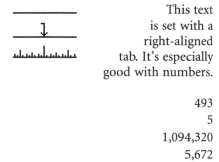

  This text
  is set with a
  right-aligned
  tab. It's especially
  good with numbers.

  493
  5
  1,094,320
  5,672

- **Centered tab:** when you create and use a *centered* tab, the text *centers* itself under the tab. As you type, the text actually moves out in both directions.

  Typically the marker has no tail at all.

This text is set
with a
centered tab.

- **Decimal tab:** when you create and use a *decimal* tab, the text aligns itself at the decimal point or at the period. As you type, the text moves out to the left; as soon as you hit the period or decimal point, any characters following the point will move out to the right.

  This is the tab to use for keeping dollars and cents in their proper columns, to keep the decimal point lined up when you have a varying amount of numbers following it, and to create the numbered paragraphs as shown on the following pages.

  Typically the marker has no tail, but a little dot next to it.

1. This number was set to a decimal tab.
2. There is also a left-aligned tab to start the text.
3. The column of numbers below is using the same decimal tab.

45.9

123,453.0056

.53

1.02

Here are the first-line indent and tab set-ups for several common ways of arranging numbered blocks of text.

1. This is the way text will align if you don't set any tabs at all. You type the number, a period, a space, then the text.

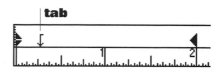

2. This is the same as above, but the text starts with a tab. Tabs are important with proportional type because spaces are not always the same, so characters won't align very well without them.

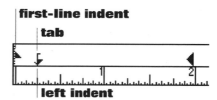

3. Now, to create this example, set the *first-line indent* at the far left. Set the *left indent* marker where the text should align.

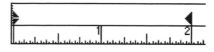

4. When you hit the **Return/Enter** key, the cursor will return to the **first-line indent**. As the text *word wraps,* it will align with the *left indent marker.*

5. Also set a *tab* directly on the left indent marker (as shown above). This allows you to tab over *to begin the first word of the text* so the first word aligns with the rest of the word-wrapped lines.

6. If you *don't* set a tab at that left indent marker, the text will look like this paragraph, where the first word is not aligned with the rest of the text.

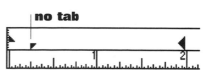

7. Now, that hanging paragraph works very well—
   it keeps everything nice and neat. A problem
   arises when the numbers get past ten. Have
   you ever noticed this happen:

   8. Text.
   9. More text.
   10. Uh oh—notice the periods and the text—
       they are no longer aligned! That extra digit
       in the **10** bumped everything over.

8. How to solve that? Well, your *first-line indent* should
   be *all* the way to the left.

9. Since the numbers have
   a period after them, you
   can set a *decimal tab* in far
   enough from the left margin
   to allow space for the largest
   number you will type. If you have
   no decimal tab available or you're
   not using a period, set a right-aligned
   tab; it'll do the same thing.

**decimal tab (or use
a right-aligned tab)**

10. Set your *left indent marker* where you want all the text to align.

11. Set a *left-aligned tab* directly on the indent marker (as shown).

12. Now, you have to do this: Before you type the first
    number, hit the Tab key; this will send the cursor to
    the decimal/right-aligned tab. Type your number;
    the number will line up on its right side.

    Now hit the Tab again to send the cursor to where
    the text will align. *As you input the text,* it will word
    wrap back to where you set the left margin (in the
    example, the left margin is the bottom half of the triangle,
    set at the .5 inch mark).

    When you hit the Return/Enter key, the cursor will go
    back to the far left where the *first-line indent* is (which
    in this example is the top half of the triangle), and you can
    begin again. Piece o' cake, right?

Widows and orphans.

Never leave widows and orphans bereft on the page.

Now obviously these terms aren't referring to bereaved widows and orphans such as some of us are ourselves—no, these are actually traditional, technical, typographic terms.

When a paragraph ends and leaves fewer than seven characters (not words, characters) on the last line, that last line is called a **widow.** Worse than leaving one word there is leaving part of a word, the other part being hyphenated on the line above.

A gentle joyousness—a mighty
mildness of repose in swiftness,
invested the gliding whale. Not the
white bull Jupiter swimming away
with ravished Europa clinging to
his graceful horns; his lovely, leering
eyes sideways intent upon the maid;
with smooth bewitching fleetness,
rippling straight for the nuptial bower
in Crete; not Jove, not that great
majesty Supreme! did surpass the
glorified White Whale as he so divinely
swam. **widow**

On each soft side—
coincident with the
parted swell, that but
once leaving him, then
flowed so wide away—
on each bright side,
the whale shed off en-
ticings. **an even worse widow**

■

When the last line of a paragraph, be it ever so long, won't fit at the bottom of a column and must end itself at the top of the next column, that lonely line is an **orphan.**

...Moby Dick moved on, still withholding from sight the full terrors of his submerged trunk, entirely hiding the wrenched hideousness of his jaw. But soon the fore part of him slowly rose from the water; for an instant his whole marbleized body formed a high arch, like Virginia's Natural Bridge, and warningly waving his bannered flukes in the air, the grand god revealed himself, sounded, and went out of sight. Hoveringly halting, and dipping on the wing, the white sea-fowls longingly lingered over the agitated pool

orphan

that he left.

With oars apeak, and paddles down, the sheets of their sails adrift, the three boats now stilly floated, awaiting Moby Dick's appearance.

In long Indian file, as when herons take wing, the white birds were now all flying towards Ahab's boat; and when within a few yards began fluttering over the water there, wheeling round and round, with joyous, expectant cries.

Herman Melville, *Moby Dick*

Avoid leaving widows and orphans. Sometimes you may need to rewrite copy, or at least add or delete a word or two. Sometimes you may have to add or delete the spacing between the letters, words, or lines, depending on which application you're working in. Sometimes widening the margin just a hair will do it. But it must be done. Widows and orphans on a page are tacky.

See what I mean?

Hyphenations and line breaks.

Avoid more than two hyphenations in a row.
Avoid too many hyphenations in any paragraph.
Avoid stupid hyphenations.
Never hyphenate a heading.
Break lines sensibly.

It's amazing how often silly line breaks show up. A line break is simply that—where a heading or sentence breaks off at the end of a line.

This is more often critical in headings or in short blocks of text than in long manuscripts, although even in lengthy text you can find those classic cases, like hyphenating the word *therapist* so it becomes *the-rapist.* We've all seen strange hyphenations like turn-ed, or-phans, occuren-ce. Some, obviously, are downright wrong. Not only are they wrong, they're a gross sign of unprofessionalism. Watch them. Don't rely on your software package to do it the best way. Use a dictionary to verify any word that looks a bit odd. Read the lines carefully; even if a word is broken properly, pick up on any instances where there may be a split second of confusion, ambiguity, racism, sexism, stupidity, etc., resulting from breaking the line at that particular point. If there is, fix it. Notice how awkward these sentences are (these actually came back from a typesetter):

SRJC is an open-access cam-
pus.

Any prospective or interested stud-
ent can contact the Instructional Office.

Almost as bad as dumb hyphenations are too many hyphenations in a row. Sometimes you can't avoid hyphenating, but it's never necessary to hyphenate three times in a row, or six of the eight lines in a paragraph. In those cases, you really must adjust something.

Often, too many hyphenations are the result of using a justified alignment (text aligned on both sides of the column, as this is) on a line that is too short for the point size. If you can't possibly left-align the text, try rewording, adjusting letter or word spacing if that's possible, kerning (see page 29), widening the margin, or adding spaces before the offending word on a justified line to bump it down to the next line.

Never hyphenate a word in a headline

Any headline can be broken at a logical point. Even though you may have no hyphenations in a headline, insensitive line breaks can still make your text awkward or ambiguous. Generally, group lines of a heading into logical grammatical sections. Which of the following would be more appropriate?

<table>
<tr><td align="center">Jimmy's Lemonade
Stand</td><td align="center">Jimmy's
Lemonade Stand</td></tr>
<tr><td align="center">Parade in the Bay
Area was a Success</td><td align="center">Parade in the Bay Area
was a Success</td></tr>
<tr><td align="center">The Theater presents Don
Quixote de la Mancha</td><td align="center">The Theater presents
Don Quixote de la Mancha</td></tr>
</table>

Watch line breaks in body text as well

Most of the text you create is flush left with a ragged right margin. Try to keep the right margin as even as possible, for the visual effect as well as for smoother reading—it can be bothersome to have lines ending at radically different points. This means you may need to bump words from one line down to the next line, or occasionally rewrite copy to adjust the lines.

Few things are pure, and they are seldom simple; and of all the impure and unsimple things in this world which befog and bedevil the minds of men, their ideas about women deserve to take first place.

— *Oscar Wilde*

Few things are pure, and they are seldom simple; and of all the impure and unsimple things in this world which befog and bedevil the minds of men, their ideas about women deserve to take first place.

— *Oscar Wilde*

Simply bumping the word 'and' from the first line to the second (by inserting a couple of spaces before the word) rearranged all the following lines to give a smoother right margin. Then I also aligned the name Oscar Wilde.

*L*eading, or linespace.

Keep the linespacing consistent.

Linespacing within a paragraph should be consistent. We often set an initial cap or a word in a larger point size than the rest of the text. This affects the linespacing, or leading (the space between the lines of type); if even one letter or word is larger, the linespacing adjusts to fit the larger character(s), creating uneven spacing.

The history of the term leading (pronounced *ledding*) may give you a better grasp of what leading itself accomplishes and how you can best adjust it.

Until the early '70s (yes, the 1970s), most printed type was set in hot metal. Each letter—each and every little letter—was cast onto a tiny piece of lead *backwards* so when it printed the letters would be facing the right direction. All these letters were lined up in a row, with other tiny pieces of blank metal stuck between the words to separate them. Even the newer linotype machines (which composed these little pieces of type whole lines at a time instead of one letter at a time) used the same principle. Between each line of type another strip of blank lead was inserted to separate the lines—this was called the *leading.*

Now, the type was measured in *points,* just like most of the type on the computer (72 points per inch). The leading was also measured in points. If the type was **10** points high and the little piece of lead inserted between the lines was **2** points high, then the **2** points was *added onto* the point size of the type and the leading was called **12** point. Got that?

10 point type on
—————————————— — *a piece of lead 2 points thick*
2 points of linespace
makes 12 pt. leading

Typically, a standard unit of measure for the leading between the lines is 20 percent of the point size: in the example on the previous page, the type is 10 point, the leading would be 12 point. (Some software manuals call the percentage 120 percent, which is the same as adding on the 20 percent.)

What all this boils down to is that when you type on the computer, you usually get an automatic 20 percent leading (that's **auto leading**). When a word or character is made larger, it automatically comes with more leading. This creates an awkward look to a paragraph, as then one line has more space after it than the others. For instance, if you use 12-point type, the auto leading is about 14 (about 120% of the point size). But when you insert a 24-point initial letter into your paragraph, the leading for that one line automatically bumps up to about 29.

It's usually possible to correct the linespacing, depending on the software application you're creating it in.

In this example,
the first letter is larger and
disrupts the even linespacing
of the rest of the paragraph.

This paragraph also has
a large initial cap, but the
leading has been adjusted.

- If your application allows you to adjust the leading, then select the entire paragraph and reset the leading to what it originally was for the *smaller* type.
- Sometimes you can adjust the leading, but it won't let you set it less than the auto leading for the larger size, the one that's disruptive. In that case you'll need to adjust the linespacing for the entire paragraph to match the *larger* type size.
- If you're having difficulty fixing the leading in a page layout program, you may find it easier to set the initial cap in its own text block and move it in next to the rest of the text as a separate unit.

- In some of the less sophisticated programs, you can't adjust the linespacing at all. But you can sneak this trick in: select one of the blank spaces between the words on a line; change the point size of the blank space to the same size as the large initial cap or word that's causing all this trouble. You'll have to do this separately for each line in the paragraph to make all the linespace consistent.

Adjust leading with all caps

You'll find extra, awkward leading between lines of all capital letters (on those rare occasions when you use all caps!). That's because capital letters have no "descenders"—those parts of the lowercase letters g, j, p, q, and y that drop below the rest of the letters. To tighten up the leading, figure out what the auto leading is (120% of the point size). Then set the leading to less than that. For instance, the auto leading for 36-point type would be about 43; reset it for less than 43. Usually on all caps you can actually reduce the linespace to less than the number of the point size of the type; e.g., 36-point type and 34-point leading—try it! Notice that the example below is 18-point type with 17-point leading, or linespace.

TOO MUCH LINESPACE

(18-point type; Auto leading)

LINESPACING ADJUSTED

(18-point type; 17-point leading)

The same is true of a line, generally a headline, that has few descenders. Lacking descenders, lines with no visual interruption in them can create space that looks larger than necessary.

Too much spacing

(18-point type; Auto leading)

Better spacing

(18-point type; 17-point leading)

Adjust the spacing between paragraphs

To have more space between paragraphs on a typewriter, our only option was to hit the carriage return twice. You've probably noticed in computer typesetting that this turns out to be an excessive amount, giving a clunky look to your paragraphs. Most software applications that use type, such as word processing or page layout programs, have a means for you to separate paragraphs by as much or as few points as you would like.

For instance, in some applications you can add a few points in a box usually called something like **after.** These few points *after* mean that whenever you press Return/Enter, those few points will be *added onto* the leading used in the previous paragraph before going on to the next paragraph. If you are using 10-point type with 12-point leading, you can add 5 points after, creating about half a linespace between paragraphs. The text you are reading here is set 10 / 13 with 6 extra points between the paragraphs.

It is redundant to indent the first line of paragraphs if you are setting extra space between them. Use one or the other: either indent or use extra linespace. But do always use *something* to separate the paragraphs visually or the text becomes difficult to read.

Justified text.

Justify text only if the line is long enough to prevent awkward and inconsistent word spacing.

The power of a word processor is so much fun that it's easy to go overboard. The tendency is to try to do all those things we couldn't do on a typewriter, and one of the most common things is to justify all the text (that is, to align it on both margins, like this paragraph). On a few kinds of typewriters it was possible to do this with a great deal of trouble, and heaven forbid if you made a typo and had to go back later and correct it. But with these magic machines, a push of a button and the entire body of text aligns itself. It's irresistible.

Resist it. The only time you can safely get away with justifying text is if your type is small enough and your line is long enough, as in books where the text goes all the way across the page. If your line is shorter, or if you don't have many words on the line, then as the type aligns to the margins the words space themselves to accommodate it. It usually looks awkward. You've seen newspaper columns where all text is justified, often with a word stretching all the way across the column, or a little word on either side of the column with a big gap in the middle. Gross. But that's what can happen with justified type. When you do it, the effect might not be as radical as the newspaper column, but if your lines are relatively short you will inevitably end up with uncomfortable gaps between some words, with other words all squished together:

"A traveller! By my faith, you have great reason to be sad: I fear you have sold your own lands to see other men's; then, to have seen much and to have nothing, is to have rich eyes and poor hands."

W. Shakespeare
As You Like It

When the space between the words becomes greater than the space between the lines, it creates what are called "rivers" running through the type.

When your work comes out of the printer, turn it upside down and squint at it. The rivers will be very easy to spot. Get rid of them. Try squinting at the example on the previous page.

Here is a general guideline for determining if your line length is long enough to satisfactorily justify the text: the line length in picas should be about twice the point size of the type; that is, if the type you are using is 12 point, the line length should be about 24 picas (24 picas is 4 inches—simply multiply the number of inches by 6, as there are 6 picas per inch).

Justified text was the style for many years—we grew up on it. But there has been a great deal of research on readability (how easy something is to read) and it shows that those disruptive, inconsistent gaps between the words inhibit the flow of reading. Besides, they look dumb. Keep your eyes open as you look at professionally-printed work (magazines, newsletters, annual reports, journals) and you'll find there's a very strong trend to align type on the left and leave the right ragged.

Isn't that an odd thing to read as you see this whole book justified? But it's just like the choice to use all caps: when you choose to justify type, you must realize you are choosing that *look* and sacrificing the most effective word spacing. Depending on the project, one may be more important than the other. For this book, I wanted the *look* of the justified line and I felt the line length was long enough to give me a minimum amount of awkward word spacing (although I must admit I still find the uneven word spacing irritating, even on this length of line; I can't have everything, they tell me).

Hanging the punctuation.

Hang punctuation off the aligned edge to eliminate any visual interruption of the text.

Hanging the punctuation is particularly important in larger sizes of text, such as headlines, or in quoted material no matter what its size. The easiest way to explain the concept is by example. Notice how the quotation mark, below, visually interrupts the left alignment of the text. The first line appears to be indented rather than flush left.

> **"When I get a little money,**
> **I buy books.**
> **If there is any left over,**
> **I buy food and clothes."**

Desiderius Erasmus

I adjusted the same block of text, below, to keep the left alignment visually intact—I *hung* the quotation mark.

> **"When I get a little money,**
> **I buy books.**
> **If there is any left over,**
> **I buy food and clothes."**

Desiderius Erasmus

Notice in the example below how even something as small as a period can create a visual misalignment.

> **Thou art thy mother's glass**
> **and she in thee**
> **Calls back the lovely April**
> **of her prime.**

William Shakespeare

Below, I hung the period off the right side to preserve the strength of the alignment.

> **Thou art thy mother's glass**
> **and she in thee**
> **Calls back the lovely April**
> **of her prime.**
> *William Shakespeare*

Squint at any text that has a strong flush alignment and notice where the alignment is broken with punctuation. Look at hyphens, periods, commas, single or double quotation marks, bullets—anything that creates a slight break in the visual continuity. Then hang it.

Inserting *non-breaking spaces* is one way to hang punctuation in a short block of text. Both of the examples in this chapter were adjusted that way. In the first example, after I set the type and noticed the distraction, I inserted an *em space* at the beginning of each line. An em space is like an em dash—it takes up a space about the size of a capital letter M in that font and size (see page 19 for information on hyphens and dashes).

In the second example, I inserted a *thin space* at the end of each of the first three lines. I added two thins after the by-line, since the by-line is a smaller point size (ens, ems, and thins are proportional to the size of type). A thin space takes up about one-fourth the amount of room as an em space.

It can be difficult to find an em, en, or thin space on a PC. So another alternative is to type the same punctuation at the end of each line (in the example above, type a period at the end of the first four lines) and then apply the style "Reverse" to the punctuation you don't need (the first three lines).

Some applications allow you to pick up the letters and marks, one by one, and place them wherever you like. Occasionally it may be easiest to set the offending line in a block of its own and manually hang the entire line. Whichever method you use, hanging the punctuation is obviously one of the last touches of detailing to do in a document. But it really must be done.

Serif and sans serif.

Serif type is more readable and is best for body text;
sans serif type is more legible and is best used for headlines.

Type can generally be classified into two major groups: serif and sans serif. Those little marks at the ends of the strokes of the letter are serifs. If a font doesn't have those, it's called "sans serif," because "sans" means "without."

Readability

Extensive studies have concluded that serif type is more *readable* in extended text than sans serif type. It's not clear exactly why; suggestions are that the serifs tend to lead the eye along the horizontal line, or that the thick/thin variations in the strokes of most serif type eases reading, or perhaps simply the fact that we all grew up learning to read from books that used serif type. Whatever the reason, it has been well-established that serif type is easier to read, particularly in extended text. Have you ever seen a novel printed in sans serif type?

Legibility

Sans serif, on the other hand, has been shown to be more *legible*. What's the difference? Well, legibility refers more to character recognition than to reading blocks of text. Put in practical terms, sans serif is easier to recognize at a glance for short little bursts of type, such as in headlines on a page or in a signage system in corporate headquarters. A full page set in sans serif may, at first glance, *appear* to be easier to read, but in the long run it proves not to be.

General use

Notice in publications how serif and sans serif fonts are used. Very typically you'll find that headlines are set in sans serif and the main body of text is set in serif. That's because it's a time-tested and infinitely variable solution.

Sans serif in text

If you do insist on setting your body text in a sans serif, keep these things in mind to improve its readability:

- Use a shorter line length (see page 46 regarding line length).

- Set not more than seven or eight words on the line (serif type can handle ten to twelve words).

- Avoid manipulating the type style to make it even less readable; i.e., as few bold or italic or outlined or shadowed words as possible.

Examples

Read this paragraph and the following one while trying to be particularly sensitive to which one feels a touch easier to read. Remember, *readability* becomes more important in lengthy text, such as a book or thesis paper, rather than in a paragraph or two of advertisement copy, but you can probably get a sense for it even in these short blocks.

When the term *legibility* is discussed, it's referring to display type, such as headlines or signs. Read the following headlines, noticing which one is more distinguishable at a quick glance. Of course, you can *read* both of them, but once you become aware of the subtle differences in readability and legibility, you begin to have a clue as to how important the selection of a particular typeface can be to effective communication.

For Sale   For Sale

Combining typefaces.

Unless you have a background in design and typography, never combine more than two typefaces on the same page.

Never combine two serif fonts on the same page, and never combine two sans serif fonts on the same page.

When all those typefaces are staring at you from the Font menu and all it takes is a click of a button to change from one to the other, it's hard to keep yourself under control and not make the page look like a ransom note. Try.

You can't go too wrong if you keep it down to two typefaces in a document. A particularly good combination is to use a sans serif for headings and a serif for the body copy (see the previous chapter). Now, within each typeface, it's fine to make some of it bold or italic or playful occasionally (try to keep the style you choose consistent with the purpose and meaning of the text).

But you should never (unless you've had design and typography training and really know what you're doing) combine two sans serif typefaces on the same page, like Avant Garde and Helvetica. Without going into a lot of design theory, the basic principle is that there is not enough contrast between the faces—they are too similar to each other and set up a subtle conflict. The combination will make your page look tacky, unprofessional, and dumb.

Combining two serif typefaces can be done more easily, but again, it takes some training to understand how to do it effectively.

If you have no background in design or typography, then it is very safe to stick to two typefaces, one serif and one sans serif. Even though you may be saying to yourself right now, "I'm not designing anything anyway," you are. Every time you turn on your computer and create a document to be printed, you're designing the page that's going to come out. If it's a newsletter, a poster, an ad, a thesis paper, an essay, or even a letter to Grandma, you are designing that page. And there's no reason not to make that page look good.

■

Helvetica and Avant Garde do not have enough contrast between them to look good together on one page. Notice the subtle differences in the shapes of the letters: Avant Garde is very geometric, while Helvetica has more classic shapes.

Helvetica

This creates a situation where there is neither *concord*, where all elements are working together, nor is there *contrast*, where elements are set up intentionally to contrast and strengthen each other. What results is *conflict*.

Avant Garde

Notice how the two sans serifs above compete with each other—they have some similarities and some differences, but not enough of either to work effectively together.

Strengthen the contrasts

When combining typefaces, don't be a wimp. Contrast with strength. If one face is light and airy, choose a dense black one to go with it. If one face is small, make the other one large. If you set one all caps, set the other lowercase.

Avoid weak contrasts, such as a semi-bold type with a bold type; avoid combining a script with an italic; or combining large type with almost-as-large type. Put some chutzpa into it!

# Miscellaneous.

Just a few asides that are important but don't rate their own little chapters.

- Use italic and bold as you would rich desserts—they're fine occasionally, but easy to overdose on.

- The traditional, standard format for A.M. and P.M. is *small caps,* which we couldn't do on a typewriter so we were taught to type them all caps. When set in all caps, though, the letters are very large and attach too much importance to themselves. Now we have the means to set them properly: type the letters in *lowercase;* select them; choose "Small Caps" from your style menu—most applications that use type have this option. (Small caps turns *lowercase* letters into capital letters that are not much bigger than lowercase itself.) There should be a space after the number and periods after the letters: 8:35 A.M.

- Regarding punctuation and parentheses, remember that the sentence punctuation goes *after* the closing parenthesis if what is inside the parentheses is part of the sentence (as this phrase here). That goes for commas, semicolons, and colons also.

  If what is inside the parentheses is an entire statement of its own, the ending punctuation should be inside also, as in the paragraph above regarding small caps.

- When placing more than one column of text on a page, be sure to align the first *baselines* of each column. The baseline is the invisible line the type sits on, and when two blocks of text are next to each other, it is critical that the first lines across the columns align.

- Don't be afraid of *white space!* (It's called white, even if the paper is black; it just means the space where there is no element printed on the page.) The area on the page that does not have text or graphics on it is just as important as the area that does. You may not be conscious of it yet, but your eyes are aware of it and how it's affecting everything else on the page. Don't be afraid to have wide margins, empty space before or after a major heading, or a short bit of copy tucked up in the upper left instead of spread out in the middle of the page. That's one of the greatest differences between a clean, professional, sophisticated look and an amateur look—the professional is not afraid to leave white space.

- When you place text inside a box, don't crowd it. Leave plenty of room on all sides. Generally the ideal is to have the same amount of space on all four sides, visually. If you are leaving more space on one or two sides intentionally, then make it obvious.

> **This text is crowded, thus making it unappealing to read.**

> **This text has more breathing space, thus making it more readable and inviting.**

- When typing numbers, never use the lowercase L (1) for the number one (1), nor the capital letter O for a zero (0). Besides the fact that they have different shapes, the computer reacts to them differently; if you'll be doing any sort of calculating, the computer will get very confused if an L is found in a list of numbers.

- Make a conscious effort to be consistent. If a heading is aligned left, then align left all the headings. If a heading is 18-point bold, then make all the headings 18-point bold. If a page number is on the bottom outer margin, they should all be there. Etc. etc. etc. Look for consistency in tabs, indents, fonts, punctuation, alignments, margins on all sides, etc.

- When listing items, as in a résumé or contents box, use a bullet of some sort rather than the hyphen or asterisk. The hyphen and asterisk were fine on the typewriter when we had no other option, but now we can use the standard bullet (•), or any of a great variety of others: ☙ ♥ ❑ ☛ ■ (these come from the font Zapf Dingbats).

- Avoid abbreviating whenever possible. Rarely is it necessary to abbreviate St. for Street or Dr. for Drive. In body text, avoid words like lbs. for pounds or oz. for ounces (something like an order form, of course, is different).

  When possible, spell out the name of the state as well. If you are going to abbreviate a state within an address, then at least do it right: states are now all abbreviated with two capital letters and no periods. California should never be abbreviated as Ca, Ca., or Calif. It looks uneducated, or at least old-fashioned.

- In headlines, the punctuation often appears unnecessarily large, placing too much visual emphasis on itself. Commas, apostrophes, quotation marks, periods, etc., should all be reduced a point size or two.

"Everything must end; meanwhile we must amuse ourselves."

—*Voltaire*

12-point text; no adjustments made.

"Everything must end; meanwhile we must amuse ourselves."

—*Voltaire*

12-point text; 10-point quotes and punctuation; punctuation hung.

■

- When you select a word to change it into italic, be sure to select the space *before* the word, as well as the word itself; don't select the space *after* the word. Italic fonts take up less space than roman (non-italic) fonts. This, in addition to the fact that they slant to the right, can sometimes create a distracting bit of extra space before the italic word unless you also italicize that space and thus make it smaller. Yes, it's subtle.

- On a typewriter we were taught that a paragraph indent should be five spaces, so we would always set a tab for that paragaraph indent accordingly. Now we can set a first-line indent, right? But the size of that five-space indent is no longer appropriate with the professional, proportional type we are now using—it is a bit large and clunky-looking.

  Traditional typesetting standards set a paragraph indent of **one em** (a space equal to the point size of the type being used; that is, in 12-point type an em space is 12 points wide). Visually, this is roughly equivalent to two spaces, or the width of a capital letter M. If your program does not allow you to specify points for indents, just use a sensitive approximation.

  Really, this is true—check the paragraph indents in any book on your shelf (except a computer book produced within the last five years).

Quiz.

In the following text there are over a dozen mistakes that need editing. They may be typos, inconsistencies, bad line breaks, wrong hyphenations, widows or orphans, or any of the myriad items mentioned in this little book. See how many changes you can suggest for making the piece look more professional. A few suggestions are on the following pages.

The Solace of Travel

To the untravelled, territory other than their own familiar heath is invariably *fascinating*. Next to *love*, it is the one thing which *solaces* and *delights*. Things new are too *important* to be neglected, and *mind*, which is a mere refection of *sensory impressions*, succumbs to the *flood* of objects. Thus lovers are *forgotten*, *sorrows* laid aside, *death* hidden from view. There is a *world* of accumulated feeling back of the trite dramatic *expression* -- "I am going *away*".

THEODORE DREISER

Sister Carrie

· wimpy contrast of fonts

wrong and bad line break

underline is too close and too heavy

The Solace of Tra-vel

· needs kerning

To the untravelled, territory other than their own familiar heath is invariably *fascinating*. Next to *love*, it is the one thing which *solaces* and *delights*. Things new are too *important* to be neglected, and *mind*, which is a mere refection of *sensory impressions*, succumbs to the *flood* of objects. Thus lovers are *forgotten*, *sorrows* laid aside, *death* hidden from view. There is a *world* of accumulated feeling back of the trite dramatic *expression* -- "I am going away".

THEODORE DREISER

Sister Carrie

linespacing is inconsistent

· wrong fonts

too much space after the period

misspelled word

wrong quote marks

· period belongs inside quote

should be an em dash with no extra word spaces

· widow

unnecessary to set this all caps; calls too much attention to itself.

· these two items need a stronger visual connection with each other; they are also too large for their purpose.

avoid underlining. besides, it is redundant to underline and italicize.

· too many words italicized

· too many hyphenated lines

· lack of contrast or concord

· line length is too short for justified text.

# *P*ossible alternative.

This is but one of a myriad of possibilities for setting this prose.

The Solace of Travel

To the untravelled, territory other than their own familiar heath is invariably fascinating. Next to love, it is the one thing which solaces and delights. Things new are too important to be neglected, and mind, which is a mere reflection of sensory impressions, succumbs to the flood of objects. Thus lovers are forgotten, sorrows laid aside, death hidden from view. There is a world of accumulated feeling back of the trite dramatic expression—"I am going away."

Theodore Dreiser
Sister Carrie

You know my methods. Use them.

— *Sir Arthur Conan Doyle*

*L*ist of Appendices.

The following appendices discuss how to create typographic characters, foreign characters, subscripts, and superscripts on a personal computer in various software applications.

*A*ppendix A: **Accessing characters**

*How to access alternate characters with PC printers
and software.*

IBM computers were not originally created for designers and typographers. It has only been in the past few years that they have been pushed to act as design stations. Thus it is not always a straightforward proposition to access the alternate typographic characters, such as real quotation marks and em dashes, from your PC. There are several key issues:

1. Is the character you want included in one of the fonts you have available?

2. If it is, how do you choose the character from within your particular software package?

In these appendices we'll look at both issues in turn—first a general discussion of character availability in printers and fonts and then a look at a number of popular word processing and desktop publishing programs to see how you can access the alternate characters in each.

Unless the character you want is available in the font you're using or one you can switch to, or can be built from characters that are available, the chances are slim that you'll be able to print it.

(The one exception to this dependence on your fonts' character collection is WordPerfect 5.1. WordPerfect 5.1 has the ability to generate any of the 1500 characters it supports on virtually any laser, dot matrix, or inkjet printer. I'll discuss WordPerfect in a later section.)

Of fonts and character sets

Just which characters are available in the fonts you're using depends on the **character set** included in the font. A character set is the collection of characters that make up a font. Different fonts vary greatly in the characters they include.

A character set is usually composed of the characters available on your keyboard plus some additional, alternate ones (some specialty fonts have only symbols and no regular keyboard characters).

There are a number of "standardized" character sets in use with PC fonts. Unfortunately, many of these commonly used character sets simply do not contain the most useful typographic and foreign characters. Some sets are very small, like the ASCII Set, containing only keyboard characters. Some, like the Roman-8 Set, have more foreign characters but lack typographic symbols. Some, like the GEM International Set, contain everything you're likely to need.

Of monitors and printers

Now, it's important to understand that the monitor and the printer are separate machines (yes, I know you knew that). The software has to talk to each machine separately—the software sends one message to the monitor and sends a different message to the printer. The message to the monitor displays the characters you see on the screen (the screen font) and the message to the printer prints the characters on the page (the printer font). Unfortunately, *the character set used by the monitor may be different than the set used by the printer.* In that case, what you see on the screen is not what you get on your printed page.

If you're using the fonts that are built into your printer, whether it's a dot matrix, inkjet, or laser printer, you're probably stuck with the character sets that are included with those internal printer fonts, and those character sets are often quite limited. If you use add-on fonts such as cartridge fonts or soft fonts (which are available for most kinds of printers) you may be able to select fonts that contain the characters that are important to you.

To figure out whether the characters you want to use are available in the fonts and with the printer you are using, you can either 1) study your font and/ or printer documentation, which should list the supported characters, or 2) use the method described in the next subsection to print yourself a chart.

Using your software to access special characters

Like printer fonts, your software has a master list of all the characters that it knows how to use, *which is confusingly also called a character set.* There's also a numbering system to select the supported characters. When you tell your software that you want a particular character by pressing the right key or keys, the software sends the character number to the printer. If the character set of the *printer font* matches the character set used by the *monitor,* everything works and you get the character you intended. This usually happens with the standard keyboard characters, which are the letters, numbers, and symbols that are often called the basic ASCII characters.

The problem begins with the special symbols that don't appear on the keyboard. Your software probably supports at least another 127 "extended" characters beyond the standard keyboard set, but the collection of these special characters supported by your software may differ completely from that included in your printer font. Your software should list all the characters it supports, and give you a key combination (like Alt 132) to get each one. *Sometimes, though, when you use that number you will see one character on the screen, but a different character may print because the printer supports different extended characters.*

Therefore, getting the special characters you want takes experimentation and may be frustrating. The first step is to try to find the characters you want in the character set supported by your software (and listed in its manual or in these appendices). Use the software's character numbering system to put the character into your document. Then print it. If you get your character, great. If not, check your printer or font documentation and see if you can find another character number for your character. Try inserting that number into your software (usually this is done with the Alt key and the numeric keypad—see the following appendices pertaining to your particular software). The character may not look right on your screen, but it might print correctly.

Some special fonts contain different characters than the ones you normally use, even replacing all the standard keyboard characters. If you want to use a specialty font (like Zapf Dingbats), your font documentation or your software manual should tell you how to get the characters in that font.

But the easiest thing to do is to create your own chart of the character sets.

Create your own character set charts

The only infallible and actually the very easiest way to always know which characters will print on your particular printer with your particular software and with your particular fonts is to create your very own particular charts of the character sets.

Here is a way to make the chart:

- Start a new document.

- Set up tabs for two columns.

- In the first column, type the numbers from 0 to 256.

- In the second column, directly across from each number, hold the Alt key down and type the same number (press Num Lock and use the numeric keypad). If you are using Windows, type a zero before the number.

Sometimes you will get a beep or perhaps no character at all will appear, especially for the first 32 numbers—that's okay. It just means that the software or the monitor cannot create a character for that key combination. The printer may still create something, though.

At this point your chart should look something like this (although the characters you see in your second column may not be the same as the ones shown here):

126	~
127	Δ
128	Ç
129	ü
130	é
131	â
132	ä

- Print that page. The first column print as the numbers you typed, but the second column will turn into the characters that will actually print in that font on that printer using that software.

- If you have fonts from other vendors, highlight the entire page of text, change the font, and print it again. If you have other software, recreate the page in the other software and print it. If you use other operating systems, reprint the page under the other operating systems. If you use other printers, reprint the page through the other printers. This is the only foolproof way to get exact proof of which characters will print.

- The code numbers 33 through 126 will always (unless you use a specialty font) generate the standard characters you see on the keyboard. All the other numbers have been utilized or not utilized in different character sets with no standards whatsoever.

Use macros to access your favorite characters

Although the methods for accessing special characters described in the following appendices are fairly straightforward, you don't want to have to use them for every cedilla, bullet, or dash. Most of the programs described have their own methods for creating macros that can reduce the steps you need to access any character to a couple of keystrokes. Once you have a set of macros to access your favorite characters, you can keep a chart of them taped next to your computer for ready reference.

The following appendices

The discussions in the following appendices cover DOS-based software, Windows software, and GEM-based software separately because software in each environment tends to use the same character set. For each environment a general discussion about supported characters is followed by information about specific programs that differ from the general picture.

Appendix B: **DOS-Based Software**

Generic information on how to access alternate characters with DOS-based software.

For technical reasons (and maybe, sheer laziness), most **DOS** software uses only the 256 characters of the IBM Extended Character Set. The IBM Extended Character Set is the basic collection of characters built into the monitor itself, whether you're at the DOS prompt or within most PC applications. The advantage of using this set is that the characters you select from it will be represented properly on your screen.

The IBM Extended Character Set is numbered from 0 to 255. The numbers 0 (zero) through 31 include special control characters and some strange symbols beloved of programmers. The numbers 32 through 126 are the basic keyboard characters. Above 126 are the so-called "extended" characters, including foreign letters, symbols, line drawing characters (why so many?), and typographic marks (why so few?!).

Unfortunately for anyone trying to produce professional-looking documents, the IBM Extended Character Set skimps on important typographic marks. There is no real ellipsis character (…) or curly quotes (single or double). There are no copyright or trademark symbols. There is a round bullet (•, 7), a square bullet (■, 254), and a triangular bullet (▶, 16). You can use the minus sign as an em dash (—, 196).

To insert any of the non-keyboard characters into your document:

1. Press the Num Lock key to toggle the numeric keypad on.
2. Press and hold the Alt key.
3. Using the numeric keypad, type the number for the character you want.
4. Release the Alt key.

In addition, some programs have alternative ways of inserting several of the most useful special characters from the IBM Extended Character Set. The following pages take a look at some specific DOS programs.

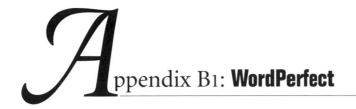

*A*ppendix B1: **WordPerfect**

How to access alternate characters with Word Perfect.

WordPerfect goes far beyond most DOS programs to make a vast range of characters available relatively easily. If you're using WordPerfect 5.1, it will even "manufacture" the right character for you if the character doesn't exist in your font or printer. It does this by sending a graphic image of the character to the printer. If you're using an older version of WordPerfect, you can still create many characters by combining elements of characters that are available in your fonts.

When you want to access a character that's in the IBM Extended Character Set, you can use the method described on the previous page (Alt key plus a character number). However, WordPerfect's character set is so much more extensive than the IBM Extended Character Set that you'll normally want to use WordPerfect's own methods for accessing characters.

The WordPerfect manual has an appendix that contains a complete listing of approximately 1500 supported characters. The characters are grouped into different sets, such as a Typographical Symbols Set (Set 4) and a couple of Multinational Symbols Sets (Sets 2 and 3). Each character is identified by its Set number plus a character number within the Set.

Compose feature
Use WordPerfect's Compose feature to either specify a Set and character number for the character you want, or to combine character elements to create a new character. The latter is primarily used to create foreign characters and is discussed in detail on the following pages.

To access the Compose feature, first press **Control V**. Then, to select a character from the WordPerfect character set, supply the Set number, a comma, and the character number. For example, to insert an em dash into your text:

1. Press **Control V**.
2. Then type **4,34** (including the comma).
3. Press the **Enter** key.

Alternate characters in WordPerfect:

"	Control V 4,32	open double quote
"	Control V 4,31	close double quote
'	Control V 4,29	open single quote
'	Control V 4,28	close single quote
–	Control V 4,33	en dash
—	Control V 4,34	em dash
…	Control V 4,56	ellipsis
•	Control V 4,0	round bullet
▪	Control V 4,2	square bullet
☐	Control V 4,38	empty square box (ballot box)
fi	Control V 4,54	ligature of f and i
fl	Control V 4,55	ligature of f and l
©	Control V 4,23	copyright mark
™	Control V 4,51	trademark symbol
®	Control V 4,22	registered trademark symbol
°	Control V 6,36	degree sign
¢	Control V 4,19	cent sign
/	Control V 6,6	fraction bar (slash / ; fraction bar /)
¡	Control V 4,7	inverted exclamation point
¿	Control V 4,8	inverted question mark
£	Control V 4,11	monetary pound

Accent marks in WordPerfect

When you want to insert foreign characters or accent marks into your text, you can find the character in the WordPerfect character sets (in the appendix of the manual) and use the Compose feature as described above. However, there's another method that may be easier. Use Compose (Control V), but type a keyboard symbol suggesting the accent mark, followed by the letter that will receive the accent. For example, to insert an **é** into your text:

1. Press **Control V**.

2. Then press **'** (the typewriter apostrophe).

3. Type an **e**.

4. You don't need to press Enter.

5. To get an uppercase **É**, press **Shift e** rather than just **e**.

Accent	Press
é	Control V 'e
ž	Control V vz
ç	Control V ,c
Ç	Control V ,C
â	Control V ^a
ċ	Control V .c
è	Control V `e
ū	Control V _u
ą	Control V ;a
å	Control V @a
ø	Control V /o
ñ	Control V ~n
ü	Control V "u

Subscript and superscript in WordPerfect

To create subscript and superscript text in WordPerfect, use the Font Size feature: **Control F8**, **S**. Then press **P** for superscript or **B** for subscript.

There are two ways to use the Font Size feature:

- You can type your text first, block it (Alt F4 or F12), then change it to subscript or superscript by using Font Size.

- Alternatively, you can change the Font Size first, then type the text, and then change back to normal text. (To change back to normal, press the right arrow key to move past the Font Size code.)

$\mathcal{A}$ppendix B2: Microsoft Word (DOS)

How to access alternate characters with DOS-based Microsoft Word.

Microsoft Word (non-Windows version) supports the IBM Extended Character Set. To access a character:

1. Press the Num Lock key to toggle the numeric keypad on.
2. Press and hold the Alt key.
3. Type the numeric value for the character you want.
4. Release the Alt key.

Alternate characters

" or "	*none*	open or closed double quotes
' or '	*none*	open or closed single quotes
–	*none*	en dash
—	Alt 196	em dash *(we'll pretend)*
…	*none*	ellipsis
•	Alt 7	round bullet
♥	Alt 3	heart bullet
▶	Alt 16	right triangle bullet
◀	Alt 17	left triangle bullet
▲	Alt 30	up triangle bullet
■	Alt 254	square bullet
©	*none*	copyright mark
™	*none*	trademark symbol
®	*none*	registered trademark symbol
°	*none*	degree sign
¢	Alt 155	cent sign
¡	Alt 173	inverted exclamation point
¿	Alt 168	inverted question mark
£	Alt 156	monetary pound
¶	Alt 20	paragraph symbol
§	Alt 21	section marker

Accent marks

ç	Alt	135		Ç	Alt	128
é	Alt	130		É	Alt	144
è	Alt	138		È	Alt	201
ñ	Alt	164		Ñ	Alt	165
ö	Alt	148		Ö	Alt	153
ü	Alt	129		Ü	Alt	154

Subscript and superscript in Word

Block (highlight) the text, and then use the Format Character menu to choose superscript or subscript.

Cool trick for finding alternate characters

Word 5.5 provides a utility that will print out a table of the printer font characters (the characters that will actually *print*, as opposed to the alternate characters you may see on the *screen*). This utility is on Program Disk #3 and is called **test_char.** When you run it, test_char will prompt you for the name of your printer and of the font. The printout will display only the characters above 127, since the numbers below 127 represent the standard set of keyboard characters common to all fonts and printers.

*A*ppendix C: **Windows Applications**

Generic information on how to access alternate characters with Windows-based software.

Most **Windows applications,** such as **Word for Windows, Ami,** and **PageMaker,** use the ANSI Character Set (ANSI stands for American National Standards Institute). The ANSI set includes "up to" 256 characters, with the first 127 being the familiar keyboard characters, and the rest being European letters and various symbols and typographical marks. Many of the character numbers are undefined in the ANSI set and can be used by specific applications. The separate manuals for Windows applications and for Windows itself contain appendices that list all the special characters in the ANSI set belonging to the particular software.

To access the ANSI Character Set:

1. Press the Num Lock key to toggle on the numeric keypad.
2. Hold down the Alt key.
3. Using the numeric keypad, press 0 (zero), then the number of the ANSI character you want.
4. Release the Alt key.

Limitations of ANSI Character Set

Unfortunately, although it contains the Western European letters and punctuation marks, the ANSI character set is severely limited in its selection of typographical characters. There are no real curly open and close quotes (single or double), em or en dashes, ellipsis dots, or bullets. Rather sad, considering that Windows is supposed to be the wave of the future. However, there is a block of unused numbers in the ANSI set from 127 to 160 that specific applications sometimes use for their own character choices.

Some Windows applications come with special symbol fonts that supplement the ANSI set with useful characters. Your application should document these symbol fonts, usually in an appendix.

Using the IBM Extended Character Set in Windows

The ANSI character set contains many but not all of the same characters that are in the IBM Extended Character Set, *though the two sets use entirely different numbering systems.* If there is a character whose IBM Extended Character Set you know, you can use that number to insert the character in your document *if the character also exists in the ANSI set.* Just toggle on the Num Lock and use the Alt key and IBM character number as you would in a DOS application (don't put a zero in front of the number). Windows will translate the IBM Extended Character number into the equivalent ANSI number *if the character exists in both sets;* if not, however, you will get a random character instead of the one you want.

Subscript and superscript in Windows

To create subscript or superscript text in Windows software:

1. Highlight the text.
2. Use the Text Enhancements feature from the Text menu to select subscript or superscript.

Symbol font

Many Windows applications support a special Symbol font containing many math, scientific, and Greek characters. Because the characters can differ for each software package, you need to see your software manual for information on this specialty font.

$\mathcal{A}$ppendix C1: **Word for Windows**

How to access alternate characters in Word for Windows.

Microsoft Word for Windows supports the ANSI Character Set. To access a character in this set:

1. Press the Num Lock key to toggle the numeric keypad on.
2. Press and hold the Alt key.
3. Using the numeric keypad, press 0 (zero), then type the number of the ANSI character you want.
4. Release the Alt key.

Alternate characters

Word for Windows has added several important characters to supplement the basic ANSI set. *Notice the numbers listed here already include the zero.*

'	Alt 0145	opening single quote
'	Alt 0146	closing single quote
"	Alt 0147	opening double quote
"	Alt 0148	closing double quote
•	Alt 0149	round bullet
–	Alt 0150	en dash
—	Alt 0151	em dash
©	Alt 0169	copyright mark
™	*none*	trademark symbol
®	Alt 0174	registered trademark symbol
°	Alt 0186	degree sign
¢	Alt 0162	cent sign
¡	Alt 0161	inverted exclamation point
¿	Alt 0191	inverted question mark
£	Alt 0163	monetary pound
¶	Alt 0182	paragraph symbol
§	Alt 0167	section marker

Accent marks

ç	Alt	0231	Ç	Alt	0199
é	Alt	0233	É	Alt	0201
è	Alt	0232	È	Alt	0200
ñ	Alt	0241	Ñ	Alt	0209
ö	Alt	0246	Ö	Alt	0214
ü	Alt	0252	Ü	Alt	0220

Subscripts and superscripts

To create a subscripted character:

- Press **Control =** before you type the character.
- Press **Control =** after you type the character to return the following text to normal.

To create a superscripted character:

- Press **Control +** before you type the character.
- Press **Control +** after you type the character to return the following text to normal.

To change existing characters to sub- or superscript:

- Highlight the text.
- **Either** from the Format Character menu, choose Subscript or Superscript;

  Or press **Control =** to subscript the character, **Control +** to superscript the character.

*A*ppendix C2: **Ventura Publisher** (Windows)

How to access alternate characters in the Windows version of Ventura Publisher.

Ventura Publisher (Windows version) supplements the ANSI Character Set with a number of useful typographic symbols. To access any character in this set:

1. Press the Num Lock key to toggle the numeric keypad on.
2. Press and hold the Alt key.
3. Using the numeric keypad, press 0 (zero), then type the number of the ANSI character you want.
4. Release the Alt key.

Alternate characters

There are two numbers given for each character in the following chart, one labeled Decimal and the other ANSI. *Note that the ANSI numbers already include the zero.*

- Use the **Decimal** number when you are creating text in your word processor to be imported into Ventura. Enclose the number within angle brackets, like so: <169>.
- Use the **ANSI** number when you are creating text directly in Ventura in the Text Edit mode.

Symbol	Decimal	ANSI	Description
"	169	Alt 0147	opening double quote
"	170	Alt 0148	closing double quote
'	39	*just use the ' key*	apostrophe
–	196	Alt 0150	en dash
—	197	Alt 0151	em dash
…	193	Alt 0133	ellipsis

•	195	Alt 0249	round bullet
©	189	Alt 0169	copyright symbol
™	191	Alt 0153	trademark symbol
®	190	Alt 0174	registered trademark
°	198	Alt 0176	degree sign
¢	155	Alt 0162	cent sign
¡	173	Alt 0161	inverted exclamation point
¿	168	Alt 0191	inverted question mark
£	156	Alt 0163	monetary pound
§	185	Alt 0167	section marker
¶	188	Alt 0182	paragraph marker

Accent marks

ç	Alt 0231	Ç	Alt 0199
é	Alt 0233	É	Alt 0201
è	Alt 0232	È	Alt 0200
ñ	Alt 0241	Ñ	Alt 0209
ö	Alt 0246	Ö	Alt 0214
ü	Alt 0252	Ü	Alt 0220

Subscripts and superscripts

To create sub- or superscripted characters, first highlight the text. From the Text menu, select either Superscript or Superscript. That's it.

*A*ppendix C3: **Aldus PageMaker**

How to access alternate characters in Aldus PageMaker.

Aldus PageMaker can generally interpret special characters you've placed in your word processing document when you import or place text. PageMaker supports the standard ANSI Character Set used by all Windows applications when you type text directly in your publication. To access any other character in the ANSI set:

1. Press the Num Lock key to toggle the numeric keypad on.
2. Press and hold the Alt key.
3. Using the numeric keypad, press 0 (zero), then type the number of the ANSI character you want.
4. Release the Alt key.

Alternate characters

Notice that these character numbers already include the zero.

°	Alt 0186	degree sign
¢	Alt 0162	cent sign
¡	Alt 0161	inverted exclamation point
¿	Alt 0191	inverted question mark
£	Alt 0163	monetary pound
™	*none*	trademark symbol

PageMaker supplements the standard ANSI character set with special keystroke combinations to access some of the most common characters.

'	Control [	opening single quote
'	Control]	closing single quote
"	Control Shift [	opening double quote
"	Control Shift]	closing double quote

–	Control =	en dash
—	Control Shift =	em dash
•	Control Shift 8	round bullet
¶	Control Shift 7	paragraph symbol
§	Control Shift 6	section marker
®	Control Shift g	registered trademark
©	Control Shift o	copyright symbol

Accent marks

ç	Alt 0231		Ç	Alt 0199
é	Alt 0233		É	Alt 0201
è	Alt 0232		È	Alt 0200
ñ	Alt 0241		Ñ	Alt 0209
ö	Alt 0246		Ö	Alt 0214
ü	Alt 0252		Ü	Alt 0220

Subscripts and superscripts

To create a subscripted character as you type:

- Press **Control ** before you type the character.
- Press **Control ** after you type the character to return the following text to normal.

To create a superscripted character as you type:

- Press **Control Shift ** before you type the character.
- Press **Control Shift ** after you type the character to return the following text to normal.

To change existing characters to sub- or superscript:

- Highlight the text.
- **Either** from the "Type Specs..." menu, next to "Position" choose Subscript or Superscript;

 Or press **Control ** to subscript the character, **Control Shift ** to superscript the character.

*A*ppendix D: **Ventura Publisher (GEM)**

*How to access alternate characters in the GEM version
of Ventura Publisher.*

Ventura Publisher (GEM version) comes with some fonts of its own and these fonts include all the characters of the GEM International Character Set. Ventura also includes a Symbol font containing Greek, math, and scientific characters. The International Character Set has a large collection of characters, including most of the useful typographical characters and most European letters and punctuation marks. If you install new fonts into Ventura using Bitstream's Fontware or Hewlett-Packard's TypeDirector, you will get a smaller character set called the VP US Set that still contains the most useful characters with the same character numbers as the GEM International Set.

Insert special characters into your word processed document before importing the text

Normally you create your text in a word processor and then import it into Ventura. If your word processor can insert special characters into your document before you import it, Ventura will accept many but not all of those characters and print them properly.

Alternatively, you can insert the decimal number for the character from Ventura's International Character Set in angle brackets (e.g., type <197> for an em dash). When you import the text into Ventura, Ventura will replace the brackets and the number with the appropriate character.

Insert special characters directly in Ventura

To enter a special character into a document from within Ventura's Text Edit mode, use the standard procedure:

1. Press the Num Lock key to toggle the numeric keypad on.

2. Press and hold the Alt key.

3. Type the numeric value for the character you want.

4. Release the Alt key.

Alternate characters

In addition to the method of using the Alt key, Ventura provides shortcuts for creating several of the important typographic characters when you're in Text Edit mode. These shortcuts are included in the chart below:

"	Control Shift [	opening double quote
"	Control Shift]	closing double quote
'	*just use the ' key*	apostrophe
–	Control [	en dash
—	Control]	em dash
…	Alt 193	ellipsis
•	Alt 195	round bullet
©	Control Shift c	copyright symbol
®	Control Shift r	registration symbol
™	Control Shift 2	registered trademark
°	Alt 198	degree sign
¢	Alt 155	cent sign
¡	Alt 173	inverted exclamation point
¿	Alt 168	inverted question mark
£	Alt 156	monetary pound
§	Alt 185	section marker
¶	Alt 188	paragraph marker

You can use Ventura's Auto Adjustments feature to automatically change typewriter quotation marks (") into open and close curly quotes (" "), and double hyphens (- -) into an em dash (—) when you import documents from your word processor.

Accent marks

ç	Alt 135		Ç	Alt 128
é	Alt 130		É	Alt 144
è	Alt 138		È	Alt 201
ñ	Alt 164		Ñ	Alt 165
ö	Alt 148		Ö	Alt 153
ü	Alt 129		Ü	Alt 154

Subscript and superscript

To create subscript or superscript in Ventura's Text Edit mode, highlight the text section and then select Subscript or Superscript from the Assignment List that appears on the left side of your screen.

Alternatively, you can insert codes into your word processor document before and after the text you want changed. Insert <^> for superscript and <v> for subscript. Insert <D> *after* the sub- or superscripted text to turn it back to normal.

Guidelines.

The following is a compendium of the guidelines established in this book. You might want to check through them each time you complete a publication.

❏ Use only one space between sentences.

❏ Use real quotation marks.

❏ Check the punctuation used with quote marks.

❏ Use real apostrophes.

❏ Make sure the apostrophes are where they belong.

❏ Use en and em dashes where appropriate.

❏ Use the special characters whenever necessary, including super- and subscript.

❏ Spend the time to create nice fractions.

❏ If a correctly-spelled word needs an accent mark, use it.

❏ Don't underline.

❏ Never use all caps in body text; rarely use it in heads.

❏ Kern all headlines where necessary.

❏ Never use the space bar to align text.

❏ Use a one-em first-line indent on all indented paragraphs.

❏ Use a decimal or right-aligned tab for the numbers in numbered paragraphs.

❏ Leave no widows or orphans.

❏ Never have more than two hyphenations in a row.

❏ Avoid too many hyphenations in any paragraph.

❏ On every line of text in the document, watch all line breaks carefully. Be sensible.

❏ Keep the line spacing consistent.

❏ Tighten up the leading in lines with all caps or with few ascenders and descenders.

❏ Adjust the spacing between paragraphs; rarely use a full line of space between paragraphs in body text.

❏ Either indent the first line of paragraphs or add extra space between them—not both.

❏ Never justify the text on a short line.

❏ Hang the punctuation off the aligned edge.

❏ Use serif type for body text unless you are going to compensate for the lower readability of sans serif.

❏ Never combine two serif fonts on one page.

❏ Never combine two san serif fonts on one page.

❏ Never combine more than two typefaces on one page (unless you've studied typography). So the gist is: if you're going to use more than one face, use one serif and one sans serif.

❏ Use italic and bold sparingly.

❏ Use proper punctuation with parentheses.

❏ Align the first baselines of juxtaposed columns.

❏ Encourage white space.

❏ Don't crowd text inside a box—let it breathe.

❏ Be consistent.

❏ Use some sort of bullet when listing items, not a hyphen.

❏ Avoid abbreviations.

❏ Use small caps for A.M. and P.M.; space once after the number, and use periods.

❏ Reduce the size of the punctuation marks in headlines.

❏ Set the space *before* an italic word also in italic.

❏ Don't be a wimp.

*I*ndex.

This book was produced on a personal computer using the software package Aldus PageMaker 4.01.

Main type families used are the Minion Expert Collection and Folio, both from Linotype-Hell.

Design and production by the author.

About the author.

Robin Williams is a part-time instructor at Santa Rosa Junior College in Santa Rosa, California. After many years of teaching graphic design and typography and coordinating the Design Graphics Program, she discovered the Macintosh. It didn't take long to switch from t-squares-and-triangles-and-rubber-cement-and-rubylith-all-over-the-place graphics to turn-off-the-switch-and-the-mess-is-all-cleaned-up graphics. Robin now teaches desktop design, electronic typesetting, and related Macintosh courses at the college and through her own training company for individuals and businesses.

Robin has written other books, including *The Little Mac Book*, *PageMaker 4: An Easy Desk Reference* (Mac and PC versions), *The Mac is not a typewriter*, and *Jargon: an informal dictionary of computer terms*, all published by Peachpit Press.

More from Peachpit Press . . .

The Little DOS 5 Book
Kay Nelson

All you need to know about DOS 5, organized concisely and written in plain English. The book is packed with plenty of tips as well as an easy-to-use section on DOS commands that explains things with everyday, practical examples. Also covers DOS basics, working with files and directories, disk management, and more. (160 pages)

LaserJet IIP Essentials
Cummings, Handa, and Whitmore

A complete guide to HP's most inexpensive laser printer. The book covers configuration and use of the IIP with major word processing, database, spreadsheet, and desktop publishing programs. It includes a special section on fonts, explains the options for upgrading the printer with PostScript cartridges and memory boards, and covers special topics such as envelope and label printing. (340 pages)

The LaserJet Font Book
Katherine Pfeiffer

This book doubles as a buyer's guide to LaserJet fonts and a tutorial on using type effectively in your documents. Hundreds of LaserJet fonts from over a dozen vendors are displayed, accompanied by complete information on price, character sets, and design. The book includes scalable fonts for the LaserJet III printer, as well as bitmapped fonts used by the LaserJet II, IID, and IIP printers. (450 pages)

The Little Laptop Book
Steve Cummings

Get on the fast track to notebook and laptop computing. This book covers choosing a laptop, protecting your laptop from theft and damage, hot tips on applications and utilities, printing on the road, and telecommunication. (192 pages)

Letter to a Computer Novice
Lawrence Magid

An introduction to personal computers that assumes no prior technical knowledge. The book demystifies computers and computerese, giving you the lowdown on hardware, software, buying and setting up a system, networks, and online services. (160 pages; available 1/92)

Mastering Corel Draw, 2nd Edition
Chris Dickman

This book provides beginning lessons and advanced tips and tricks on using CorelDRAW 2. Tutorials include manipulating shapes, grouping graphics, text shapes and paths, fills and color. Appendices cover file exports, slide creation, and techniques for speeding up the program. A special color section displays award-winning drawings along with tips by their creators. (398 pages, plus disk)

DeskJet Unlimited, 2nd Edition
Steve Cummings

This book is an in-depth guide to the HP DeskJet family of printers. It explains how to use these printers with major word processing, spreadsheet, graphics, and desktop publishing programs. It also includes extensive information on fonts (including downloading and converting from LaserJet format), troubleshooting, DeskJet programming, and tips on practical tasks such as printing envelopes and label sheets. (393 pages)

The *Publish* Book of Tips
Eckhardt, Weibel, and Nace

A compilation of over 500 of the best tips from five years of *Publish* magazine, the leading magazine for desktop publishers. The tips cover all the major desktop publishing software and hardware products, including Ventura Publisher, PageMaker, WordPerfect, CorelDRAW, Windows, PostScript, fonts, laser printers, clip art, and more. (500 pages)

TypeStyle: How to Choose and Use Fonts on a Personal Computer
Daniel Will-Harris

The purpose of this book is to help the average user understand the basics of type: how to choose the right typeface, which typefaces mix well together, etc. It covers not only the mechanics, but also the psychology of type. The book includes over 50 full-page examples featuring fonts from Bitstream, the world's largest type vendor for personal computers. (368 pages)

Ventura Tips & Tricks, 3rd Edition
Nace and Will-Harris

This book was described by Ventura President John Meyer as "the most complete reference for anyone serious about using Ventura." Packed with inside information: speed-up tips, "voodoo tricks" for reviving a crashed chapter, ways to overcome memory limitations, etc. Features a directory of over 700 products that enhance Ventura's performance: utilities, fonts, bulletin boards, clip art, monitors, style sheets, and user groups. (760 pages)

WordPerfect for Windows with Style
Daniel Will-Harris

This book explains how to get the most out of the remarkable new WordPerfect for Windows program. In many ways, WordPerfect for Windows is the equal of such highly regarded desktop publishing programs as PageMaker and Ventura. Author Will-Harris is renowned for his humor and insight into the desktop publishing scene, from graphics programs to laser printers, fonts, and style sheets. (400 pages)

PageMaker 4: An Easy Desk Reference
Robin Williams

This is a reference book rather than a tutorial, organized to answer any PageMaker question as quickly as possible. Three columns are labeled "If you want to do this," "Then follow these steps," and "Shortcuts ▼ Notes ▼ Hints." Includes a tear-out shortcuts chart and an industrial-strength index. (784 pages)

Jargon: an informal dictionary of computer terms
Robin Williams

At last—a computer dictionary with definitions you can actually understand. Most terms are not only defined, but are explained in relation to their function and interaction with other terms. Illustrated. (96 pages)

The Mac is not a typewriter
Robin Williams

This book is similar to *The PC is not a typewriter* but is written specifically for Macintosh users. (72 pages)

Peachpit Press, Inc.

2414 Sixth Street
Berkeley, California 94710

800.283.9444
510.548.4393
510.548.5991 FAX

*Your satisfaction
is unconditionally guaranteed
or your money
will be cheerfully refunded!*

Order Form

800.283.9444 or 510.548.4393
510.548.5991 fax

Quantity	Title	Price	Total
	DeskJet Unlimited, 2nd Edition	23.95	
	LaserJet IIP Essentials	21.95	
	The LaserJet Font Book	24.95	
	Letter to a Computer Novice (avail. 1/92)	12.95	
	The Little DOS 5 Book	12.95	
	The Little Laptop Book	14.95	
	The Little WordPerfect Book	12.95	
	The Little WordPerfect for Windows Book (avail. 1/92)	12.95	
	The Mac is not a typewriter	9.95	
	Mastering Corel Draw, 2nd Edition (with disk)	32.95	
	PageMaker 4: An Easy Desk Reference (IBM edition)	29.95	
	The PC is not a typewriter	9.95	
	The Publish Book of Tips	24.95	
	TypeStyle	24.95	
	Ventura Tips & Tricks, 3rd Edition	27.95	
	WordPerfect for Windows with Style	23.95	
	Jargon: an informal dictionary of computer terms	9.95	

Tax of 8.25% applies to California residents only.
UPS ground shipping: $4 for first item, $1 each additional.
UPS 2nd day air: $7 for first item, $2 each additional.
Air mail to Canada: $6 first item, $4 each additional.
Air mail overseas: $14 each item.

Subtotal	
8.25% Tax (CA only)	
Shipping	
Total	

Name

Company

Address

City	State	Zip

Phone	Fax

❏ Check enclosed   ❏ Visa   ❏ MasterCard

❏ Company Purchase Order #

Credit Card Number	Expiration Date

Peachpit Press, Inc. ▾ **2414 Sixth Street** ▾ **Berkeley** ▾ **CA** ▾ **94710**
Your satisfaction is unconditionally guaranteed or your money will be cheerfully refunded!